THE
TAKE
OVER

Joe,

I am honored to call you
my friend! You are an
amazing guy! Thank you!

THE TAKE OVER

The Ultimate Mind Booster

THIS PRACTICAL GUIDE WILL HELP YOU ADD POSITIVE
SUCCESS FILES TO YOUR MIND ALLOWING YOU TO LIVE A
MORE FULFILLING, POSITIVE, AND HAPPIER LIFE.

GEORGE "GK" KOUFALIS
BRAD A. MODRICH

Published by

George "GK" Koufalis
P.O. Box 3157 Bethlehem PA 18017
www.chaseyourvisions.com

Brad A. Modrich
P.O. Box 3324 Allentown PA 18106
www.bradmodrich.com

ISBN 978-0-578-47097-9
Printed in the United States of America
Library of Congress Control Number: 2019902818

*If you truly want to be successful, you must be willing
to help as many people as possible without expecting anything in return.
Do things for people who will never be able to repay you.*

CONTENTS

ACKNOWLEDGMENTS

George "Gk" Koufalis

I would like to express my gratitude to everyone in my life. That's family, friends, and loved ones. That extends to anyone who supports me in a positive way. I'm truly blessed and grateful to have such amazing people in my life and circle of influence. Thank you all who supported my first published book and the other businesses I own. Without you, I couldn't do what I do. Thank you to my co-author Brad Modrich – we have been friends for over 15 years, business partners for 8, and I look forward to our lifetime friendship. When I asked you to collaborate on creating the ultimate self-help book, you were 100% in. I'll never forget the true friendship you showed to me in 2009 when most turned their backs on me. Because of that, you are like family and I'm beyond excited to be partners with you on this venture. Thank you for trusting me on this project. 100 years from now, we won't be here, but this book we left behind will.

I'm even thankful to those who didn't support me along the way or were not fans of my work. This allowed me to be challenged and tested which forced me to work even harder and become a better version of myself. For all the people who crossed my path for a reason, a season, or a lifetime, thank you from my deepest part of my soul. This book is dedicated to all of you. Once again, thank you to my grandma that passed on July 22nd, 2014 in Greece. Thank you for your kindness, love, unselfish generosity and adopting me as a toddler. The love and kindness you displayed to me are being used in my life's work. Since your passing, I've used your passing as my eternal motivation to be the best I can. It's my obligation to you for paving the way. Thank you to my mother Irene; I know you did your best as a single mom. You taught me that with the right belief and immediate action, anything is possible.

Last but not least, a special dedication to Ernest Thomas Mantore Jr., my fiancé's father. He unexpectedly and tragically passed away as I was literally writing chapter 13. His passing reinforced the importance of helping others chase their dreams and leaving an impact with this one shot at life. Everyone loved Ernie, and he was a such a devoted father to his son Tommy and my fiancé, his daughter Monica. His sudden death has become even more of a driving force for me to write this book more than ever. It once again proves that no matter what we plan in life, it won't necessarily go as planned, but we must always re-adjust, push through, and overcome. Ernie, I know you're looking down smiling. Thank you for creating Monica, she's been a blessing!

Brad A. Modrich

First I would like to start off by thanking my family. To my wife Jan Costa-Modrich for putting up with my stubborn behind for the past 17 years and supporting me through thick and thin – you are my rock. To my son Brian, I can't even begin to tell you how proud I am of the man you've become, you make me a better father and a better man and last to my daughter Natalie, my beautiful brown-eyed girl who has become such a beautiful and smart young lady – you are my everything. All three of you have been my purpose for being so driven. I would also like to give thanks to my two amazing sisters Monica Modrich and Jennifer Modrich-Zughbi. The two of you have always been my biggest fans, my loudest cheerleaders, and my strongest supporters since I came into this world.

I would also like to thank all my friends, colleagues and business associates that have supported me on my journey. I appreciate you all and there's nothing but gratitude for our friendship and I look forward to continuing to grow with all of you. Special thanks to my co-author George "GK" Koufalis. Our friendship has only gotten stronger over the past 15 years. You have been a guardian angel that constantly supports me and encourages me to be great and step outside of my comfort zones. Words can't express the level of gratitude that I have for you, and I know that you have my loyalty forever. Thank you, my friend, for being yourself and paving a path for myself and others to be successful.

Lastly, this book is for the people out there that know deep down inside that they are destined for greatness but do not have the foundation nor the belief in themselves. Alas, I was once one of those people. Trust me, as a knucklehead kid from the East Side of Allentown that dropped out of high school and became a convicted felon… YOU CAN DO IT.

Trust the process, be disciplined and
TAKE ACTION. ~ B.A.M.

INTRODUCTION

Life is a series of choices and those choices create the life we live. Many of us go through life making choices without even knowing what they are. It is as if we are on autopilot and just going through the motions. Many times, we don't realize that there is a ripple effect from these decisions. The ripple effect will either work to help your life be successful or it will make your life more difficult. If you never become aware of this ripple effect, you will never implement a system of choices to create what you dream of. The power of manifestation will never be unlocked. Learning to unlock the powers within you allows you to break barriers that most never will.

Reading this book is going to help you unleash all the powers already within your grasp. Have you ever wondered, how did my life get to this place? Why didn't my dreams come true? Will I ever succeed? Can I still get to the next level? Will I ever be happy? Will I ever make more money? Will I ever meet the right partner? Well if you're reading this, I'm happy to tell you that this book is for you and more importantly, if you are reading this, it is because you are ready to start winning or further grow your current version. For everything in this book, we both utilized pulling ourselves from some dark and lonely places to a world of abundance and happiness. We decided we had to share our personal growth tools with those we cared about, you.

This is edition 1 of *The Takeover* which contains life's 20 crucial tools to help you have a transformative change in your life. These are things we were not taught in school. These are things that all highly successful people live by. When we first learned these skills which we like to call golden nuggets, they shifted our thinking and it felt like we found a secret vault reserved for the ultra-successful. Our goal is that you become fully self-aware and start making choices with a purpose behind them. That you'll truly realize the thoughts it takes to get from point A to point B in the journey of life. When you decide to utilize all the knowledge expressed in this book you will organically change your thinking. This undoubtedly will lead to a new feeling which will elicit a new action. That will without question create a new action. Your life will re-start the ripple effect in a new forward direction of value.

This book is for the 5% of the world that are the savages! You may not even know you're a savage yet, but you will one day discover this. Only a small percentage will understand all the information and utilize it properly. These 5% are the people who have been taking hits from life and always get back up to fight another day. What's going to be different after you read this book is that you'll be hitting back a lot harder! Also, in the last round, you'll be the winner! Get ready for the takeover and you will never think the same way again...

TAKEOVER 1

INNER POWER UTILIZATION

I believe that humans are incredibly powerful even beyond measure, and that includes you reading this too! The accomplishments that they have developed during this time on earth are unbelievable. All things created that we know started through a thought. This shows us that everything starts as a formless substance in the mind. The book you're reading was a thought that GK and I had on a plane to Dallas for my network marketing companies' yearly convention. As the flight was in progress, I decided to take out my note pad on my phone and start writing. I didn't wait for everything in my life to be perfect – I acted and it was massive action. I then shared that thought with Brad because I knew he was on the same mindset level. His thoughts started to manifest as he took action with me and made this book a reality.

We are what we think we are. In life, you will make a choice and you become that choice. Keep in mind that thoughts without action are not going to create the dreams that float around in your mind. If there were 5 grasshoppers on a porch and 1 decided to jump off the porch how many grasshoppers would be left on the porch? The answer is still 5, just because 1 "decided" to jump, it didn't necessarily take action. "Deciding" alone is not action, and that's where people fall short. Most people make decisions all day long which are only in their mind – they're not fully committing to the action step. If you want to grow your career, grow your bank account, change your body or create the best possible life for yourself, you will have to take action. There is no other way around it – it falls on you!

Many of you don't realize how powerful you are because society has sold you on the idea that you're not good enough, smart enough, pretty enough, or fit enough. You have fallen victim to the socially acceptable excuse for failure. There is a lot of money in telling and selling this. I'm here to tell you "don't believe the hype" as that is far from the truth. All of that noise is designed to falsely influence you to believe that. Your only competition is what is staring at you in the mirror. Ultimately, if you're happy, that's all that matters. Mohammad Ali was the self-fulfilling prophecy. He told the world that he was the greatest boxer of all time. He did this before he became a professional boxer. Self-belief can make you, and self-doubt can absolutely break you. Your thoughts are real things that when given energy, you will bring that thought to life. Today is the day when you decide you can achieve anything you set your mind to. Today, you're going to take action like never before.

The key points – You're powerful beyond measure and if you take action, you can achieve what your mind believes. Also, don't allow the world to convince you that you are not good enough. Start believing in yourself and follow through. This is your time on Earth and it's your chance to shine, why should you stay dull, there is no good reason for that. What the mind can conceive and believe, it can most certainly achieve. Now go out there and manifest your thoughts by taking action!

TAKEOVER 2

WORK ETHIC

We are all born with our natural given talents. Most of us don't even know what they are. It's our duty to find out what gifts we possess. Many who have come and gone before us have proven that talents can be grown to an unbelievable level. The bad news is that talent alone doesn't win in life, it takes hard work too. It's a proven fact that those who hustle the hardest win in life. Just look at your social media pages and you'll see those individuals that consistently hustle are showing the most success. Coincidence? Of course not! You can't lie to the hustle, it pays in the effort. Hustle is also the most tangible thing you can do to change the outcome of what disappoints you the most in life. In my life, I've come across some talented people who didn't have the drive to work hard and grind in the journey of success. I know many others who are more talented than us authors, but we are more "successful" because they can't out-hustle us.

When it comes to hustling, the first thing you must do is put one foot in front of the other. Too many times I have seen people fail because they wait for the perfect time or they will wait for the perfect opportunity. Put one step in front of the other and then repeat, and as long as you are moving forward and progressing, you're on the right path. Hustlers don't stop – they keep moving and over time their forward progression is what gets them to what they want and where they want. A mandatory key to success is to have a great work ethic. If you want to succeed in life, you must have a great work ethic.

Having a poor work ethic can hold you back from getting a new job. It can hold you back from missing an opportunity and it will prevent you from having the life you have always dreamed of. Also, a person's work ethic can tell you a lot about the person. If one has a good work ethic, you can almost always assume that this person is going to be reliable, trustworthy, effective, and do what they say they are going to do. A person's work ethic is a huge part of their character. Even if you hate what you're currently doing, know in your heart that it's temporary and still be the best at it because how you do one thing is how you do everything.

If you look at any iconic athlete from Michel Jordan, Kobe Bryant to Wayne Gretzky or Tom Brady, besides being extremely talented, they all possess a phenomenal work ethic. Having this type of drive and determination to be the best at anything will require massive amounts of effort. This, in most cases, is what stops 95% of people. You must maintain a strong work ethic regardless of what is going on in your life. It has been said that success and failure will always leave a trail. What does your work ethic say about you? Are you always on time? Are you consistent? Do you finish projects all the way to the end? Work ethic is a very important part of one's character. For me, as a founder of multiple companies, I'll take somebody who has an amazing work ethic and great attitude over somebody that is extremely talented with a bad work ethic and a bad attitude.

Throughout life, you'll see people with natural born talent that never tap into it, and to us that's a tragedy. You have one shot at this thing called life. Use it or lose it because there is an expiration date on all of us. We are committed to helping people we coach who are stuck by reinforcing they have talent and it takes hard. We don't know a single person who became successful without hard work. Everything that has been built on this earth from scratch was because of hard work and patience. Patience goes hand in hand with hard work. Most people will only scratch the surface of success. Most people get a few roadblocks or non-believers telling them no and they quit. If you're reading this, I need you to tell yourself right now, that you're not most people. If it's not patience, it's complaining. People will complain about how things are rather than adjusting to the way they are. Adjusting in life is one of your biggest tools for success.

Every initial plan that gets us started doesn't take us to the finish line, so learn to adjust and not complain. The successful people around you have no sympathy for your complaints. The only people who will listen to complaints are the other people who are frustrated in life and not getting ahead. Complaining is a waste of energy. You can do better things with your energy and mind. Positive creates positive and negative creates negative, and complaining is negative! Just look at your social media posts from people that you encounter; there is always that one person who year after year complains publicly. It's 5 years later and their life is in the same spot. No hustle and always complaining. If this sounds like you, today is your new start.

The key points – you must hustle and you must make it a daily promise to work harder. This is the only way to close the gap from where you are, to where you want to be. Be patient, as success takes time and one must adapt through life's unexpected challenges along the way. Remember that complaining has no benefits. So, we urge you to work hard, be patient, adapt, and stop complaining. Go out and be somebody, because anybody can be a nobody. It doesn't take anything to be nothing, be something!

TAKEOVER 3

VISUALIZATION

I'm a big believer that you can't hit a target that you can't see. Everything in my life that I have accomplished, I did twice. Once in my mind and once for real. If you can't see yourself get that promotion, get that new car, get that nicer home, get that significant other you want or see yourself being what you're thinking about, you will never get there. People become and produce what they think of the most. Even career criminals serving long prison sentences had to see themselves committing the crimes they did. They thought about the plans and how they would do it. This works for good and bad. You must make a choice which direction you're going to be thinking towards. At this very second, it's not important where you are in life, but it's important what direction you're going towards.

Direction will change your life through the thoughts that lead you to that direction. If you and another person are both in Pennsylvania today, but your mind wants to be in California and you go in that direction, you'll be in California and that person will still be in Pennsylvania. So, see it in your mind first, then take the direction towards that to accomplish what you want. If you're thinking about things that will take you in the wrong direction, quickly change those thoughts. Remember that energy flows where attention goes, and your life will always go in the dominant direction of your thoughts,

I've learned that success attracts success. For this to work, you must become more attractive. I don't mean in the physical sense. What this means is that you must talk, walk, and act like you already have accomplished what you are so eager to do. For this, it takes the mind to utilize its imagination an important trait. Just look at your children or your friends' children – they have an unlimited supply of imagination. Unfortunately, somewhere along the way, we lose our belief in ourselves and our dreams, with our imagination lying dormant. Notice that I didn't say our imagination dies because it never dies – it only sleeps. Today is that day where you need to wake that beast of an imagination back up again. As you change, the energy that comes into your life will change too.

You will attract the same energy that you put out into the universe. Birds of a feather flock together, as they say. If you are a pigeon, you will attract other pigeons. If you act like an eagle you will attract other eagles. Most people look at me and perceive me as someone who works out a lot. Therefore, many other people who work out recognize this and are more likely to engage with me in conversation. If you have confidence in your presence and a posture that tells the world you're a somebody (and not a nobody) then you will attract other successful people in your life. It's like when you buy a car and the next day you see the same model of car everywhere. Those cars where always there, you just didn't attract them because they weren't in your mind's realm. Your own neighbor or coworker may even have the same model car and you never noticed until you bought yours. You are the pilot of your thoughts, your direction, your imagination and what you attract to your life. Make a vow that today, you'll put yourself in the right mindset to create the life you want.

Brad here, the reality is, you are the director of your life. The same way that a director of a movie has a vision in their mind. You must do the same. Guess what? You have the star role in your movie. Visualize it, vividly imagine it. Let that vision be so clear that you have every little detail broken down to exactly what you want. I'd like to share something with you. I WILL own a Lamborghini Hurcan Perfromante. I know what color it's going to be, I know what the stitching on the seats is going to look like, and I even know what sneakers I will be wearing when I step out of it for the first time. I have every detail set out in my mind already. If you can see it in your mind, you can hold it in your hand.

One of my favorite books is "Think and Grow Rich" from author Napoleon Hill. This was the very first book that I read that taught me the power of visualization. It was in 2003 and I was an entry-level membership salesperson. My wife was pregnant with our daughter Natalie. I was making about $300 per week commuting to work for approximately an hour every day. It definitely wasn't all sunshine and rainbows in the beginning. I remember my wife and I having a serious heart-to-heart conversation in regard to how much money I was bringing in to the house. She asked, "is this gym thing really going to work out?" I asked her one question. "Do you trust me?" and she looked at me with a worried yet very committed look and said "Yes. Yes Brad, I trust you." I told her with absolute confidence in every single fiber of my DNA "I got this babe," and I did! I had made well over 6 figures every year for the 17 years that I was committed to my position as a Vice President for a national health club chain. Not bad for a high school dropout with a felony on his record.

Now let me explain why I was so confident in telling my wife that I got this. I already had visualized in my mind that I was going to be the person that opened up this full-service Health Club in Allentown. All I did was think about it and how my family would benefit from me being successful. It was more than me. My 'why' was greater than my 'how' and I made sure that I saw it in my mind. Every little detail. I visualized myself opening up the door for the first time and I ultimately manifested exactly what I had in my head. I remember one week actually, we were going to open this club for the first time to the public. It was November 30, 2004, at 4:00 PM and as I was walking to the front door. Something stopped me for a brief second; I have no clue what. I noticed and I said to myself, "Brad you did exactly what you said you were going to do." It all started with being able to visualize what I wanted.

The key points – You must see clearly in your mind the result you are wanting in life. You must believe and act as though you have already succeeded and possessed what you desire. You must awaken your imagination and then reverse-engineer what you want in life. I want you to see the prize and feel that it's already achieved. Take the step of using your imagination to feel how your life would be with that goal achieved. Now start acting like you are the person who achieved it and you will attract the right people and things into your life. This is your time to shine, don't waste another year being stuck. More importantly, make your decisions based on where you want to be in the following years and not where you are emotionally today. Successful people make choices based on where they want to be in the future and unsuccessful people make choices based on their current mood.

TAKEOVER 4

MIND CONTROL

Your mind will be your biggest asset or lead to your biggest demise. Everything we know in life starts as a thought. The conscious part of the brain creates thoughts. The subconscious has the job of helping prove your thought right. So, when your thoughts are those of doubt, fear, or any thoughts that negatively affect your life, the subconscious will prove you right. The good news is that as easy as it works for the negative, it just as easily works for the positive, albeit with a time lag. Feelings like fear, doubt, worry are felt instantly. This creates a result just by the thought alone. Positive thoughts that lead to a better life need action behind them. Therefore, time is the biggest factor in manifesting what the conscious brain desires.

Once I understood this concept, I was able to start keeping tabs on my own thoughts. No one ever told me that I should even do that. So, it wasn't that it was hard, it was that I didn't know how. Once I became aware just like you are now, I felt like I had a new weapon in the game of life. As strange as this may sound, at times it feels like I'm stepping outside my body and looking at my thoughts from a parent's role. It was only soon after I learned this information I'm sharing with you that I experienced a breakthrough. I signed up for an entrepreneur meeting on a Thursday night at the end of March a few years ago. The night of the event came, and it was snowing in spring. It was unusually cold out and I had woken from a nap on what we know to be called waking up on the wrong side of the bed. To make matters worse, my girlfriend came home early, and I hadn't had much time to see here that week. So, the excuse thoughts were piling up fast. Everything was stacked against me and I told myself I don't want to go to the event. Immediately my brain started coming up with all the reasons I mentioned why I should stay home. I almost gave in but then I remembered what I had recently learned. I knew I had to immediately change my thoughts.

The hardest challenge in a human being's life is the conquering of one's own self. I ended up going to the event and I made some great new friends and I even added a business partner to my network marketing business. This would have never been possible with my old mindset. My old brain, as I like to call it, would have passed up another great opportunity. I can't tell you how many great experiences I never experienced because of my thoughts talking me out of it.

In January of 2018, my business partner and I were invited to a fitness seminar in order to showcase our fitness apparel line. I was told we would be the only vendor there and the competitors would be in a closed room for a few hours but would be walking out and would see the table on the way out. We felt that this was a waste of time and we wouldn't sell anything, but my new brain said "conquer your thoughts and go". I thought that something good must happen by going. To make matters worse, it was cold and raining and we were up very early on a Sunday morning. We got to the event to set up and the seminar had already started. We didn't know that only the male competitors were in the seminar room. However, the women's seminar started in 2 more hours. We sat there bored with no sales, trying to make the best of it. Believing what we always believe, it's the universe testing us for the future.

Slowly but surely, female competitors from multiple states were starting to arrive. The open hallway was soon filled with women all wearing leggings and we were selling leggings. We sold 600 dollars' worth of leggings in one hour and was the most sales we had ever done in an event for a few hours up until that point. To make matters even better, one of the female competitors reached out to me on Instagram asking how I started my own business and created success. I explained it all – I started with network marketing and sent her a short video. She not only joined my business, but she also built an impressive team and created success for her, her sister, and many others. All from one event, I tried talking myself out but with parenting my thoughts I overcame my brain and until this day, I am seeing things happening in my life due to going to that event. I urge you to always show up, even when it seems like nothing good will happen. Once you experience this new thought process as we did, you'll be excited to go somewhere that your old thinking would have thought was a waste of time.

Brad here, let me explain it to you like this. First, there's a thought, thoughts turns into feeling, feelings turn into action, and actions are what create a habit over time. Now based off of whatever the initial thought was, positive or negative, is what the end result will be. Start with a negative thought and you'll end up with the negative result. Start with a positive thought and you'll end up with a positive result.

Did you know that the human brain has over 75,000 thoughts a day? That's right, 75,000! So, if you are consistently having negative thoughts about what can go wrong and what you don't have you will ultimately have negative results that are not in your favor. That I can also swing in the other direction. If you are filling your thoughts with positive, uplifting, grateful, and empowering thoughts, there is a high probability that you were going to have some great results that will end up in your favor.

Have you ever heard the saying it's "you versus you"? This is the battle of one side of your brain talking to the other side of the brain. It's all of the negative things versus all of the positive things; this is a universal law of life. There are some simple things that you can do on a daily basis to have the positive outweigh the negative. Start with some simple questions. What are you reading? What are you listening to? Who were you communicating with the most on a daily basis? What does your self-talk sound like? What are your friends having conversations about? It is so easy to focus on the negative things in one's life or focus on the things that you do not have. Anyone can do that; it requires zero effort. It is a thought process of weak and most likely unsuccessful people. So, if you know that you need assistance in changing your thoughts and beliefs, start reading some motivational books.

GK had the great idea of adding both of our top five favorite books and podcasts in the back of the book. Listen to some podcasts, heck you can even search "motivational video" in YouTube and there will be thousands of videos that you can listen and watch to feed your mind with positive content. What you feed your thoughts with the most is what you will manifest and bring to life. GK and I are living, breathing proof.

The key points – Your mind is what has created your current reality today. It's been the sum of all your thoughts and beliefs up until this moment. What career you have, who is in your circle of influence and even what amount of money is in your bank account. It is important to re-evaluate your thoughts when they are not moving you forward. Learning how to reverse the brain's attempt to keep you comfortable is key. You must be more aware of your thinking as if you're parenting your mind. When it chooses comfort over growth, you must fight back and talk to yourself. I promise you, next time do what you're talking yourself out of and you'll thank us!

TAKEOVER 5

FEAR

Fear is the biggest killer of a better and more fulfilling life, and fear is just something that only exists in our minds. False emotions acting real is what I believe fear really is. Most people in their life will allow fear to hold them back. For some, it's fear of what their parents or peers will think about them. Worrying about what others think is a recipe for failure. You need to only worry about what you think and what you want in life. I didn't want to trade places with any of my friends I spent time with before I became successful. This made me realize there was no reason to need a cosigner for my dreams.

Opinions alone won't pay the bills! If it's a parent or someone you highly value and you're worried about what they think, then you should talk to them. Let them know you're about to embark on chasing after your dreams. Express that you're worried about what they think and it's holding you back. Let them know you're going to do it regardless. It may work out or it may not work out but because you respect them, you're letting them know this. Getting that off your back will allow you to leap forward.

You may be surprised by the reaction you get from being honest. Honesty can go a long way, but even if it does not, it's your time to shine no matter what.

Let's dive deeper into fear. One of the jobs the brain has is to keep us safe. When we sense fear, stress or danger we are programmed to escape that situation. If you see someone who looks sketchy walking down the street, you'll walk in a different direction. If you see a cliff as you're driving, you'll drive in a different direction. The brain makes sure we stay alive. The brain also senses fear when you're frightened in order to chase your dreams. So, although the brain helps us when it's for our life's protection, it may also stop from enhancing our lives due to not distinguishing the difference in fears. This is where the important self-awareness trait must kick in. This is where you must push through the fear and level up as the elite and successful all do.

This is Brad writing. Ask yourself this, what are my fears? Are you worried about what other people think? Are you in fear that you can possibly fail? Are you in fear of what your family will think of you? Let me put it to you like this, fear is fake, fear is not real, fear is in your head, fear isn't an imaginary thing, fear is the voice in your head. Just as we said earlier, you control your thoughts. I am speaking from experience when I say that I was always in fear that I would never be able to get my life back on track, I was in fear that I would never be able to accomplish anything of significance with my past always lurking in the shadows. It was all nonsense – if you would have asked me 20 years ago if I was ever going to write a book, I would have told you that you were out of your mind… but look at me now!

Eliminate the fear out of your life. Most of us do experience a fearsome point, and we can run from it, but we can't hide from it. One of the best techniques I've used to overcome any type of fear that I had whether it was physical or mental was leaning into it. What I mean by that is that I will I face it head-on. I'll break down the barriers in my mind and use some critical and creative thinking to overcome whatever that fear is. I highly suggest that all of you do the same. Fight your fears one-on-one. In most cases, you will see that whatever that fear was it really wasn't that bad.

The key points – If you are to be the successful version of yourself, you must not allow other opinions to slow you down or stop you. Winners have thick skin and yours is about to get thicker. Other people's opinions are none of your business. If someone is stopping you from proceeding forward in your life, you must have that talk and be confident and honest. Learn to recognize when the brain is trying to protect you from harm as opposed to holding you back because of false emotions acting real. Fear will be most people's worst enemy, but you're not most people. One thing we want to drill into your head with this book is that you're a winner and it's your time to win. PS: but you have to put the work in even more so when you're scared.

TAKEOVER 6

ENERGY

There is a quote GK and I share often, probably weekly, because it's that powerful. I also like to remind myself of these words as it helps reset me, as we all need that reminder. That quote is, energy flows where attention goes, your life will always go in the dominant direction of your thoughts. That was an eye-opening discovery for me; I can honestly say I was never the same after understanding those words. We have a friend named Brian that Brad went to high school with and I had the privilege of meeting in my bodybuilding days. He shared that knowledge with me one day in New Mexico as we were building our network marketing venture together. In a nutshell, those words mean that what you focus on grows.

When your energy is focused on opportunities, you will get more opportunities but when your energy is focused on problems, you will attract more problems. Most people who don't have a passion and thinking for chasing their dreams will have a life revolving around their problems. Learning to always focus the direction of your energy on the solution rather than the problem will allow your mind to look at the things you face differently. Here again is where self-awareness must kick in because our natural reaction is to focus on the problem when something happens to upset us. As time goes on and you improve your self-awareness, your reaction time to solution mode will get faster and faster. I still sometimes get caught up in the problem, but I live in that moment only for a short period of time and that's what makes the difference. I take a deep breath and ask myself "what is the solution?" Then I put more energy into that solution or finding it if I'm not sure what it is.

Another important thing I do when the solution is not clear is to contact someone in my circle of influence who is solution-oriented and get their input. I have a motto, "if it doesn't matter in a year, it doesn't matter at all". The truth is that problems will never go away, even when you are living your best life. If anything, you will have more problems.

Usually, problems are a good thing – it means you're growing. I once jumped in my Benz on my way to a business meeting and halfway there I realized the laptop I needed was in my Lexus. That's a good problem to have, but it's still a problem. I simply made some calls and got a colleague to bring a laptop. I didn't waste any of my day worrying about something that doesn't matter today. You must learn to protect your energy from yourself at times. Your energy and how you go about your day, literally, will dictate your life. This is the nucleus of how you operate. I know a lot of very successful people that have massive financial wealth. One thing that they all have in common is a ridiculous amount of positive energy. Now I know what you're thinking "well if I had massive financial wealth, I would have positive energy too". Well, let me be the first to tell you that these people that I know that have massive financial wealth always had a positive outlook even when they were not so wealthy. It's a pretty simple formula – the more positive energy you put out, the more positive energy you get back. It's simple math. Now let's start using your new energy ASAP!

I want to give you creative thinking exercise. Imagine that every day when you woke up you had a battery that was at 100% full of power/energy. As you go through your day you have to take some of the energy from your battery and use it for whatever you are going through in life. An example – I use 10% of my energy at the gym today. I used 5% of it helping my wife with her business plan or how about I had to give 20% to a friend that was only complaining about all of the problems in their life. Even worse, I spent 25% of my energy concentrating on problems in my own life.

That energy is a nonrenewable resource. Once you give it out to someone or something that is not helping you, it's ultimately a waste of energy. If you're going to give anything or anyone any amounts of your energy, make sure that it is used in a positive constructive way that will allow you to accomplish your goals and progress in you and your family's life. Your mind is like a container that only holds so much. If you're filling your mind's capacity with negativity, drama, and stress, there isn't any more room for the good stuff.

The key points – You must be self-aware of what you're focusing on and make sure you audit your mind. When a problem arises ask yourself what will take it fix? Will it matter a week from now? A month from now? A year from now? Usually, the answer is no. Recognize problems are a sign of you growing in life and its part of allowing you to grow. To one who much is given, much is expected of them. Money doesn't make you positive; you make yourself positive. As you become more aware of the skills, we are sharing in this section and the entire book, you will see a major shift in your life. Be sure you are self-aware of who or what you're giving your energy too.

TAKEOVER 7

ENTITLEMENT

First, we must understand our life is a gift from our maker and what we do with our life is a gift to our maker. However, understand that the world owes you nothing. Too many people are waking up like it's an accident. Like they're just here on earth to just exist. They are completely forgetting that each one of us has a purpose and we are here to find that purpose. I'm sure if you're reading this you want to know what your life's purpose is. This book was written to guide your mind in the opening to develop your best version and ultimately finding your purpose. We must produce the life we want through our thoughts and actions.

Many of us have been told we are special growing up, but when you get into the real world as an adult, the universe doesn't think you're special because you think you are. The universe doesn't hate you as many people think it may while blaming their shortcomings on life itself. It just doesn't bend its laws and we must show that we are worthy of having our dreams come true. Everyone knows that person who is always talking about life isn't fair or how someone else caused his current life situation. That is a person who mentally is not taking responsibility for their life. Until they do, they will be in the same place year after year. We all have things happen to us but it's always our choice how we respond and what we do from there. Life doesn't care about your issues. The universe cares about you doing what it takes to create the life you want. You can't cheat the universe it knows if you're really trying. You can lie to yourself, but life always knows the truth.

Once it sees you have exhausted your efforts and you're truly committed to bettering yourself, it will then manifest all your wishes. Most of the time you'll be grinding with no results. Yes, I said no results. At least not that the naked eye can see. This is part of the process and until you embrace it, you'll be stuck. It's important to spend time with other people going through the same process or that have been through that process.

They say that teamwork makes the dream work, and this is 100% true. Having support can help you understand that it's normal and you'll overcome it. If you don't have that circle of influence, go out and create it. There are people who want a better life as bad as you do out there; you just must look for them and attract them to your energy. We will attract to our lives the same energy we put out there. Just as if we half-ass something, we will get half the results. Yes, some people are born with more opportunities and have the initial advantage. I grew up in an abusive home as a kid and had a troubled life but in the end, once

I started to follow the lessons in this book, I was able to quickly catch up and surpass others who had the privileged life. Hard work will always beat privilege and even talent.

You must put in the work. Nothing is owed to you. The second that you understand those two things, I mean really understand them, watch how quickly you can change your world. When you start thinking about yourself and you focus on helping others, entitlement will soon disappear. On top of that, you will start to get a feeling of serious accomplishment once you start earning the rewards from the work. Hands down this is one of the biggest confidence boosters in the world. Then once you started to get momentum, you can truly be an unstoppable force, but you MUST put in the work and you MUST stop thinking that you are owed something.

I remember clearly getting passed over for a promotion that I thought was owed to me. Looking back on it I now, I was wrong. I worked for a performance-based company and when the opportunity came for the promotion, I was performing at a subpar level and the end result did not merit a promotion at that time. In my head, I kept saying things to myself like, "you know how much you did for this company" or "look at how many managers you promoted out of your club". These were all thoughts of entitlement. I kept referring to the past knowing that the company I work for consistently focused on the present production and present results.

So, let me break this down for you because it actually turned into a double negative. I had negative thoughts about why I didn't get the promotion based on "entitlement" so I was mad at the company and then I made matters worse by holding this resentment and concentrating on the problems, so I stopped performing at my current position. I didn't hit my sales quota that month nor did I attain my bonus. Why? All because I thought something was owed to me. If I would have applied some of the chapters in this book, I would've held myself accountable, I would've been self-aware, and I would not have had a sense of entitlement. Which in turn, what would have happened that month that I didn't get promoted, I would have at least hit my sales quota and bonus. Now go out there and start working like you never have before, it's in you and you know you can, you will, and you MUST! Nothing is owed to you, but everything is available to you.

The key points – We cannot go through life feeling the universe owes us something because we were given life. We must still pave our way in this thing we know called life. There is no way to achieve your desires without focus and effort. Anything less won't give you results. At times we will feel beaten and want to wave a white flag, but that is the time we are truly being tested. It's then and only then that we will have a breakthrough. Understand, you can't change your beginning, but you always write a new ending, regardless of how bad you have had it or have it.

TAKEOVER 8

FAILURE

There is a larger majority of people who are failing than succeeding in life. There are many reasons for this and some of those reasons are simply that some people just don't have the mental ability to understand the need to be the best they can be in life. But what about those who have so much potential and never get ahead. The ones you want to shake and snap them out of their current lower level of existence. Rather than shake them, it's better to understand them and get to the core of that person. In my years of coaching, I've learned that you must peel people's layers like an onion to get to the truth of what keeps them stuck. Usually, the number 1 issue is the specific fear of failing. Most people don't realize the importance of failing or as we like to call it failing forward. Trust us as we have repeatedly failed, it will strengthen the mind and build a more powerful version of you!

Many years ago, Brad and I accepted that failure was part of the process. We realized when new got frustrated from the lack of success in our efforts, we needed to stay positive and associate with others in our circle who were also chasing success and winning. When we are failing over a long period of time, we are always honest with ourselves. Many times, we regroup and change the plan. Albert Einstein said an awesome quote that went something like this "insanity is doing the same thing over and over and expecting different results". If you're getting the same results it's time to stop the insanity and redirect your course of action.

This fear of failing is why many people never do anything, build anything, or experience anything in life worthwhile. Many live an average, mediocre, and broke life rather than learning to overcome their fears. Many of these people also have big egos and see themselves as being too good to ask for help. They don't want others to see them vulnerable or not good at something. So rather than be humbled, they decide to never grow. Many will also pretend they live an extraordinary life, especially showing off on social media to make themselves feel better amongst their peers.

I have said many times before, to me, status is buying things you don't want with the money you don't have to impress the people you don't like. We are asking you to embrace fear, make it an ally. Use it to grow and move forward while others use it to quit. Just know the pain you feel is temporary and trust me it goes away quickly when you know how amazing the end results are from overcoming it. Now the pride lasts forever, the pride in knowing that you took a shot and you will continue to work at improving yourself and accomplishing things you want.

I want to take you back to your childhood. Can you remember the first time you rode a bicycle? I can remember mine. I think I still have the scars on my knees to remind me. I remember crying because I didn't want to get on the bike by myself. I was nervous. I was scared but I got on the bike. I crashed hard! I didn't even want to get back on the bike; as a matter of fact, I didn't. I didn't get back on the bike until three or four days later because I had this fear a falling again. I got on again and I did it. I succeeded in riding the bike. I rode my bike so much after that that I wanted to be a BMX racer like in the movie RADD. However, we'll save that part for another story one day.

Remember this, nothing worthwhile ever comes easy and if it does, it never lasts. As you experience failure, you must ignore the naysayers, or they will be the nails in the coffin. That's when you're most vulnerable to outside noise and quitting. Use failure as a learning experience to progress and not experience the same failure again. But in case you do, which may happen, just keep learning and you'll eventually win.

The key points – You must understand that you're going to fail and you're going to fall, but if you allow your fears and your previous failures to dictate your future, you will be stuck exactly where you are right now. Falling victim to the fear of failure is one way to ensure an average unfulfilled comfort zone life. Failing forward is the only way to success. Failing is an opportunity to become better. If you don't experience failure, you'll never grow.

Remember failing is your friend and that friend is there to help you. It's time to be fearless and go out and get those failures that will lead to your wins!

TAKEOVER 9

SELFLESSNESS

Why do you see so many people have quick success and then fall back to where they started? I've seen this many times over – as quick as they succeed, they lose it all. The reason is that these people are going through life self-centered. They are only thinking of themselves. All they care about is the person looking back at them in the mirror. It's about how much can they gain? How will it benefit them only? We all know someone like this. They brag about what they have but never truly help anyone else. At times they even keep how they succeeded a secret from others who are trying to advance. This is exactly why those individuals although always hustling still get nowhere in life. They are always focused on benefiting themselves and no one else.

This is a losing behavior and always comes crumbling down. I see these people in my network marketing industry also. They build a team and have people that trust them and look up to them but as soon as something new and shiny comes along that benefits them, they jump ship and leave their entire team behind to fend for themselves. Eventually, people like this are exposed and they lose credibility and trust. In the end, no one wants to do business with them. If you go through life self-centered, self-focused and only worried about what the universe will give you, you'll learn the hard way, it's not the best formula for success. Actually, it will end up being your formula for permanent failure.

If you're going through your daily life manipulating things so that they serve you, it's not going to work. If you are getting ahead at the expense of others, it may give you momentum or even success, but it will be short-lived. As stated earlier, we all know people who jump from one thing to another and are always talking about the next best thing. These are the people who are not looking to help anyone but themselves. They have a mentality that is not of service and make people feel like they're transactions.

Being selfless or being of service to others is the way to truly have success in life. If you are starting a business or selling something, you must add value to people's lives or solve a problem. If you're leading other people in the workplace or anywhere for that matter, you have to dedicate yourself to the betterment of these people who are grinding away every day on the front lines. If you want your customers to love your product you must give back more than what you're asking in dollars. Universal laws don't bend and only when caring about others will others care about you. We define true character by how you treat those who can do nothing for you. I can share this with you from my own life; the more I've given in my life and the more people I've helped the more abundance I've been granted.

Brad here, a great friend and fellow leader of mine taught me this and I highly recommend that you put this somewhere that you could see every day. If you truly want to be successful, you must be willing to help as many people as possible without expecting anything in return. Do things for people who will never be able to repay you.

Being a servant leader for the past 16 years is what allowed me to be able to connect so closely with all of the people that I have managed in the past, consistently always putting their needs ahead of mine. This selfless trait throughout my career was a key factor in having such amazing teams and had the ability to create a phenomenal company culture. The people I supervised also managed their teams from the same level of leadership, becoming servant leaders. Everything begins and ends with selfless leadership.

The key points – Bottom line if you are only out for yourself you will lose. Any success you create will be short-lived. People who jump from one thing to another are an example of those who have short term success because it's all about them. We must give without expecting to receive in life. Adding value to others, focusing on giving more than receiving, and wanting to better others will give you the best chance at long-term wealth and success. You must learn to help others win and you'll win too. Zig Ziglar said it best, "You can have everything in life you want, if you will just help other people get what they want."

TAKEOVER 10

PERSONAL ACCOUNTABILITY

Y ou have to own it. All of it. Personal accountability for one's actions and disposition in life is the foundation of a person's success and failures. I Brad grew up on the Eastside of Allentown in a low-income household that survived on food stamps, block cheese, and powdered milk. Growing up, I would always hear the adults blaming the people they worked for on why they were getting paid so little. I would watch people work for years and years doing something that they didn't enjoy and not having any financial success.

As I look back now, I understand that they had zero accountability for their actions and all they would do is blame situations or other people for why they were failing. Any one of those people could have picked up a book to study, to learn a new trade or they could have easily got a new job, they could've worked two jobs, there's a grocery list of things that they could've done to change their finances, as well as their living conditions.

I would have to say that being accountable for your actions is hands-down probably one of the most important ingredients for success. Being accountable for what time you get up every morning, being accountable for staying healthy, being accountable for your personal growth, being accountable for every single action you take. If you are not happy with your job, start going to interviews. If you are not happy with your current financial situation, stop spending. Who really needs a $1000 dollar iPhone? (That was not a poke at Apple, I love all Apple Products) I think you know where I'm going with this. Take an honest in-depth look at yourself and hold yourself accountable to be the change that you want to see in your life. Accountability will only work when you look at that person in the mirror.

You must take personal accountability for your actions. At the end of the day, no one is going to do the work for you, no one is going to self-develop for you, no one is going to do anything for you. You have to be the person that takes complete ownership of their life. No longer can you make excuses. Everything begins with you and everything ends with you. It's that simple. OWN IT.

This is GK expressing my thoughts on accountability. I went through life not having full accountability in my life up until it led me to trouble with the law, homelessness, poverty, and rock bottom. Once I realized no one was going to knock on my door to save me and it was up to me and only me, I started taking full accountability for my thoughts, feelings, and actions. Once you do that, the force shifts, and your energy goes in a new direction. A new direction means a new path and a new path leads to a new outcome. We can teach you all the skills to better your life but if you're not accountable for your choices it won't work. When you skip the gym, be accountable and learn. When you're late to the important meeting, be accountable and learn. When you're late to class, be accountable and learn. When you're late to your kids' game, be accountable and learn.

You get the point... be accountable and learn. Learn what exactly you may ask, learn to stop doing what's holding you back. Here is where self-awareness kicks in and you talk to yourself and you call yourself out. Just know we are not asking you to be perfect, we are not perfect all the time. However, with proper mental tools, you can improve and be pretty darn close to perfect as someone can be.

The key points – It's your life and only you can be responsible for the outcome. It starts with taking full accountability and being honest with yourself. No matter what life throws at you knowing you ultimately have the power to choose being honest with yourself and learning from it or blaming everyone else instead. It's human nature to look for a scapegoat but until we look in the mirror and make that person we see accountable, nothing will ever change. Remember when you point a finger at someone else, 3 fingers are pointing back at you. We can't count on others to be accountable for our success, it's on us. You must be the person that takes complete ownership of your life, not 80% but 100%. No longer can you make excuses. Everything begins with you and everything ends with you. It's that simple, own it, no more excuses!

RITUALS

Y our ... in ... s ... tell you ... who y ... thin... You ... t ...

Thank you so much for taking the time to purchase my book. My purpose is to help people reframe their thoughts and to manifest the life that they want. If you could please: 1) Take a picture with the book (and send to me please) 2) Post it on all of your social media tagging me and using the #THETAKEOVER 3) If you saw value in it, please leave a review on Amazon 4) Again if you saw value, please record a 1-2min video testimonial about what you thought about the book.

...kely why you are at where you are ...ryone has rituals, good and bad. I've ...me again, tell me your rituals and I'll ...t you do repeatedly ultimately becomes ...lity. This is probably true for most of the ... health. Your finances. Your relationships. ...reer. I can keep going on here.

...r have bad rituals or none at all. If you want ...g in your life, you have to take a look at how ...ut your day. What are your morning rituals? ...exercise and nutrition as an example when I ...it my morning rituals. Obviously, you all know ...are extremely passionate about taking care of our health and w...llness. It would be so easy for us to skip the gym or eat poorly, just like 60% of the population does. I get up before the sun comes up, I immediately drink 15-20 oz of water and take my Opti Greens 50 on an empty stomach and then I will go down and do 20 minutes of some form of cardiovascular exercise.

Immediately when I'm done, I will eat a well-balanced breakfast containing high-protein, lower to moderate carbs and high-fiber. This is my ritual for the past 5-6 years. Why? 1) It's my standards, which we will get into next. 2) I start my day off every day by getting the blood pumping and fueling my body with what it needs for me to perform at an optimum level. It doesn't matter where I'm at – this is my morning ritual. Can you see how important it is for you to have positive healthy rituals? Doesn't matter how cold out it is outside, it doesn't matter how hot out it is outside, it doesn't matter what is going on in my life – this happens every single morning regardless. I'm sure you've heard many times before that people are creatures of habit. This is a basic human instinct.

This is GK adding my experience. Rituals can also be called habits. It's the things that we must do every single day or at least 80% of the time no matter what is going on in life. Rituals are supposed to help you have more wins than losses during the week which creates winning more weeks which becomes winning more months. In the end, you win the year. In the NFL, an 8-4 record can get you into the playoffs if it was a 12-game season. In life, winning 8 out of 12 months or even a 7-5 record is still a win at the end of the year. Some years, I go 12-0 and some years I go 7-5 but it's still more wins over losses and that comes down to having the proper rituals in place. Rituals are like the plays of the game practiced every day in sports organizations. You're making your own daily playbook.

We become what we repeatedly do. The best companies, sports teams, businespeople, and entrepreneurs all have rituals. They are not just waking up just hoping the right things will happen. Successful people have their calendar full of structured days. I can look at someone's schedule and tell you how much productivity they will have that year. The successful have a blueprint already of what each day should consist of. This system of rituals repeatedly over time, is what creates that breakthrough in your life down the road.

For me, I make sure that I don't grab my phone immediately when I wake up. I practice gratitude on being alive and give my mind a few minutes break before the frenzy of the day. I'll play with my dogs a few minutes and go over my significant other's day. I then do cardio for 20 minutes before breakfast and as I'm doing that, I check all my emails, texts, daily calendar, and social media platforms. At some point in the day, I'll check in with different members of my circle of influence, work out at the gym, and read 10 pages of a good self-help book or watch a self-help video.

These are my daily rituals that happen 80-100% of the time. The reason why it's not always 100% is that life throws things at you that you don't expect. Like a vacation, traveling for business, holidays and the unexpected, for example. I'm not going to tell you that you must be perfect all the time, that's unrealistic. I think some motivational speakers come across a little unrealistic making everyone feel they must be perfect all the time. I'm going to be as transparent as possible with you because otherwise you might feel that you're not living up to the standard because you're unaware that successful people are not perfect. I challenge you to make a list of 3-5 rituals that you promise yourself, you'll do, starting tomorrow. Unless you're reading this at 5 am, then start today. There I no better time than now, to start your new rituals.

The key points – It's simple, as success and failure will always leave a trail. In most cases of failing, it is because the rituals and the standards that you hold for yourself are not in line with the life that you are wanting and dreaming about. It requires discipline and the disciplined individuals are winning. This same concept can work in every aspect of your life. The rituals with your finances, the rituals with your relationships and the rituals with your health and wellness. Remember, you are what you repeatedly do. The goal is to have more wins than losses and to specifically have an outline of what your rituals will be. To do this, all you need is to start implementing a system of rituals. Your rituals will be the light as you pass through the tunnels leading you to the land of success.

TAKEOVER 12

STANDARDS

I'd like to start this with a quote from Tony Robbins that always stuck with me. "If you want to change your life, you have to raise your standards." You can absolutely raise your standards regardless of how much money you make. It's not about money; it is about mindset. You are going to notice as we start to move forward that all the topics that we are giving you will naturally start to flow through one another.

When I think about standards, there are many ways to explain how standards can affect your life. I would like to share a story with you, my wife is probably going to kill me for this one. This is Brad. My wife, Jan, was a member at the gym that I worked at as a personal trainer over 17 years ago. I must've asked her out 10 to 15 times prior to us going on our first date. This is still one of my top ten memories in my life. The reason she kept telling me no is because she had a boyfriend. I wasn't trying to hear that though. It even got to the point where she had to bluntly tell me to stop asking and to leave her alone "stop asking me, for the last time, I told you that I have a boyfriend" she said. She had a standard and there's nothing that would have made her change her mind. Her mind was set in stone because of her standard on loyalty in a relationship and she would not bend for anyone or anything. After her and her boyfriend at the time separated, she then called me to ask me out on that date that I eagerly waited for. As you can see, one of my standards is I exhaust my efforts, always going after what I want. Seventeen, great, happily married years later, we can both look back and laugh but yet still appreciate what her standards were at that time. Your standards have to be set in stone and only change them to upgrade them; lowering your standards will only hurt you in your journey.

Now, look at the standards you have. You must have standards in every facet of your life. Standards on how you dress, standards on how you do business, standards on your work ethic, and standards on your finances. If you truly want to get the most out of your life, you must elevate your standards and more importantly figure out the actions that require you to maintain the highest standards. This most likely will mean that you will have to disassociate with those individuals whose standards are below average. Remember you are some of the five people you hang out with the most.

Having high standards means that you are very specific to who you want to be and will not just settle for anyone or anything. Once you have it set in your mind exactly what you want you should not settle for anything less because when you do, that is when you create a new standard. Over time, if you have repeated that cycle, you will consistently lower your standards time and time again. Please trust us both when we tell you that there's absolutely nothing wrong with having extremely high standards. I want everyone reading this to stop for a moment and think about the standards that you have in your life. There is a standard for everything. What are yours like?

Being a Vice President of a billion dollar per year company, I had to have high standards. I had standards on the way my team looked, I had standards on the way that my team sold, I even had a standard on how they hung signs up in the clubs. It was that simple. have high standards and do not waiver from them. When you're fixated on having high standards the quality of how you operate day to day will ultimately raise the quality of your life.

When it comes to standards, most people have a challenge in raising them. Never apologize for having high standards. If the people in your life truly want to be in your life, they will rise to meet your standards. Do not go back to less just because you're impatient to wait for the best. We say this often, it is a fact, you will lose people that are close to you as you start to raise your standards. Especially, as you're taking action and progressing towards the life that you have always dreamed of. It's all a part of the process, so raise your standards today.

This is GK giving you my perception of standards. I believe that standards are a set of principles that you have in your mind as a must in your life, and you must not settle for anything less. Standards play an important role across the board in relationships with significant others, friendships, business partners, income, and just the overall quality of your life. It's knowing what you want in all aspects of your life and how you won't settle for anything subpar to those standards. For example, the significant other that I will be with must also be mentally on the same level as me and have the same beliefs for moving towards the future or else I can't date that person. My friendships must be supportive and positive and have no drama, otherwise I can't spend much time with those people. Financially, I must make x amount of dollars each year and I won't settle for anything less.

Therefore, I'll hustle multiple streams of income and do whatever it takes. Physically, I'll be as fit as I can or at least have a standard of what I want to be and always meet that standard. Mentally, I will utilize x number of hours a week on self-development. Work wise, I must be a certain job rank and no less, therefore I'll do what it takes to get promoted. These are all examples of standards that all successful people have planned out. You are in control of what life will give you. If you don't get out of life what you want, you get out of life what you truly deserve. By having solid standards, you'll get what you deserve. Ask yourself what are your standards? If you're not clear on them, I urge you as soon as you get done finishing this take over skill, write a new standard down that you're going to start to follow immediately.

Obviously, it may take some time to reach the standards but at least you know what the target is you're aiming at. You can't hit a target that you can't see. Also, if you already have standards this is the time to raise those standards don't shoot to low.

The key points – The standards we set for ourselves has a huge effect on the quality of our lives. If we settle for low standards, we will not always bring the best out of ourselves. Personal standards are most likely set from the behaviors that we choose daily. These behaviors are built upon the expectations that you have of yourself in a variety of different situations. You must look at them as performance standards. In other words, lay out the benchmarks of performance in your life. Your personal standards reflect the promises that you keep to yourself in the way that you manage your life.

There is a standard for every part of your life. Setting low standards only takes you so far on your journey towards your goal. With low standards, you will struggle. But when you set high standards, you immediately raise your expectations of what is possible and now you suddenly will expect more from yourself more from your actions and more from others. Standards are crucial for reaching the highest point in your life. It's a way to have a measurable target of what you stand for. Let's raise those standards!

TAKEOVER 13

CIRCLE OF INFLUENCE

This is GK writing right now. Originally, the circle of influence was supposed to take over number 20, the reason being that all the tools you'll learn in this book are based on you putting them into effect and you being solely in charge. However, there is one major outside factor as I like to call it the kryptonite. This is your circle of influence. It's what will push you to the top or it will sink to the bottom. Brad agreed with me that we should put it in the book now. You are 65% of the way through, so congrats on that. This will allow you to start adjusting your circle of influence before the book is over. Rather than having to do it at the end after you once you have learned all the takeover skills.

I'm sure you've heard, you are an average of the five people you spend the most time with. Throughout my life, I heard you become who you spend time with. If you hang out with five successful people, your probability of success is almost certain.

If you hang with 5 career criminals, there is a great certainty you'll be the 6th criminal. In hindsight, I realize now that a huge portion of my lack of success prior to finding my way was due to my circle of influence. Even in the Bible which was written before everyone's time reading this, it states that spending time with the wise will make you become wise, but the friends of fools will suffer. This is not a new concept. But it's a concept we somehow overlook as we go through life building relationships. I can tell you that the 5 People I spend the most time with now are totally different than the 5 people I spent the most time with 5 years ago. The people 5 years ago are totally different than the 5 people from 10 years ago.

As my life evolves all or a portion of my circle evolves with it. It must if I want to continue success to higher levels. If my circle decides to grow with me then we keep running together. If not, then I have no choice but to move on without them. I can't go backward to hang out with someone; they must meet me on the level I'm working on. I'm not telling you to wake up tomorrow and remove everyone out of your life. That's not realistic. But maybe evaluate all the people around you and start asking questions. Are these people adding value to my life? Are they pushing me to do more? Are they big thinkers? Are they positive people? Or are they negative, full of drama, content with being mediocre, gossipers, and people that hold you back? Sometimes we don't even notice it until we start hanging around people who are winning in life.

When you spend time with winners, I promise you that the conversation is very different. I suggest spending less time with people not moving in the direction you want and adding new people in your circle that are in the direction you want go towards. In my life, I feel as if I am piecing together a winning team. An all-star team that's going to win the championship game of life. To win any championship the players need to be special.

So, look at your life as if you're entering a championship game and you need the best people on your team for life's journey. Teamwork makes the dream work! For me building the right team to have the best chance of success in life happened when I started a network marketing business. On paper, I didn't have the skills to be a 7-figure earner. However, by utilizing all the takeover tools and over time removing the wrong people out of my life and adding the right ones into it, I was able to crush it. Not just in network marketing but multiple business industries.

Now I'm super protective of my energy and who can rent space in my mind. Don't get me wrong, I still will help anyone not on my level yet. I'll take a call or answer an email, but that time-sharing is very limited. At the end of the day, everyone is still a human being, and no one is better than someone else based on success. It's just about wanting different things in life and making sure we surround ourselves in the right environment for what we want in life. If you utilize the self-awareness takeover skill during your interactions with people not of your circle of influence standard, you'll be able to interact without them influencing you negatively. That's when you have mastered self-awareness and the circle of influence.

I could not agree with GK anymore; let me speak from experience. Recently in my life, I had to seriously take a look at the people I spent the majority of my time with the most, and this was a hard thing to do. As a knucklehead kid from the East Side of Allentown, you grow up having a certain sense of loyalty to your friends. Almost as if it was a "code of the streets." As I started to reflect on my past, I could see that this "code of the streets" mostly led me to getting jammed up or in trouble. I asked myself a serious question "are these people truly helping me become a better person and are they going to help me and my family progress and attain our future goals?" This was a deep question and a very serious time for self-reflection. The answer hurt a little bit, as my heart and head both knew what I had to do. I had to make some changes. This has been a pivotal point in my growth in the past four years.

I know right now you're reading this and you are thinking "those are my friends, my boy, my homie, that's my brother", and they. I do not devalue any of the friendships that I have, and I still love all of those people, but I had to surround myself with the people that had prosperity and success on their mind because that's what I must have for my family. I'm creating a legacy and if the people that are around me do not have the same thought process and goals, I must make the appropriate changes to progress. I forced myself and pushed myself out of my comfort zone and started creating new friendships with the people that had a millionaire's mindset and didn't make excuses.

Let me leave you with this, the people that really know you, will do one of two things, join you, support you and love you through this process of growth and evolution or they will hate on you and not show you any support. That was the true sign of their friendship.

The key points – There is no way of getting around it, you will share the same life qualities as the people you associate the most with. Your circle of influence with either add or subtract value from you. Circle of influence is the takeover skill that can affect your happiness, level of success, and your future because of others. You have to recognize which of those in your circle are working with you or perhaps against you. Deciding who you will spend your time with is very important and you need to reevaluate everyone in your circle and adjust things accordingly. With the right people in your circle, you can accomplish anything you want. Remember people's true colors come out as you rise higher in your quest for success. We believe that once you start to surround yourself around the right people, all the takeover skills will make you unstoppable.

GOAL INITIALIZATION

This chapter is designed to give you something that you can apply immediately. How can you ever hit the center of a target if you do not know what the target is? For the past 16 years, Brad and I have consistently had daily goals, along with monthly goals, along with yearly goals. Setting a goal will give you a structure to your life, so there's no question about it. There was a study done with the graduating class of an Ivy League college – 84% of the graduating class did not set goals nor did they have their goals written down on paper. 13% of the class set goals but did not write them down. Only 3% of the class set specific goals and had their goals written down on paper. The 13% of the class that set goals had doubled the income over the 84% of the class that did not set goals nor write them down. However, the 3% that set goals and wrote them down were making 10 times the income of the other 97% of students. There's so much power inserting goals and putting the pen to paper.

What is it that you really want? Do You want the nicer things in life? Is it a nicer car? Is it a nicer home? College for your children? A retirement plan? This is where TAKEOVER 3, VISUALIZATION, starts to kick in. GK and I both told you, you must see it in your mind before you can see it in your hand. Vision boards have always helped me with this process. So first you must know exactly what it is that you want. Now, this may change over time as you progress and your vision becomes clearer. It is all part of the process, my friend.

Now that you know what you want, I would like to share with you a very simple and effective way to start winning a day at a time. Just so you know, you are going to hear a million different ways throughout the course of your progression on how to set goals. This is what I found works extremely well for 95% of people. I have used this technique for over 16 years; I would simply call it my "to do list" every day but now I call them my "critical tasks" instead. On a side note quick, a great leader that I started to follow about four years ago by the name of Andy Frisella, did a whole podcast on this called "WIN THE DAY". FYI, Andy is a great leader and mentor he has helps me truly understand the process of winning one day at a time. Win one day at a time, then win one week at a time, then win one month at a time, then win one year at a time. FYI, this man has created multiple seven/eight-figure companies and he still, to this day, uses this technique. That solidified the process for me.

I would like you to get a good old-fashioned notebook. Every night before you go to sleep, break out your notebook and write down five things that you are going to get accomplished tomorrow. This doesn't mean you that you have to go to the grocery store and get milk. These are five things that are going to help you progress with your income, in your career, in your business, as a mother, or as a father, or as an entrepreneur. Now, this part of goal setting could be something as simple as reading 10 pages a day for your own personal and self-development. It could mean doing some form of exercise for at least 30 to 60 minutes per day in order to have a strong and healthy body. Sometimes when starting your journey, you must get some fundamental habits down before you can progress to the next level. A building is only as strong as its foundations. As you start to progress, you are successfully reading 10 pages a day as part of a habit and you're exercising 30 to 60 minutes per day because it is a part of your lifestyle and your habits. Then you could add something new to your five critical tasks and replace the reading or exercise with something else that will help you progress.

Now for the people who already have successful habits of reading, self-development, and exercise you need to be more strategic with your critical tasks. Let's say that you own your own company and you're looking to pick up 20 new customers this month, that would mean you need to average five new customers a week or you could set a daily task of getting one new customer per day. By the end of the month, you would have surpassed your goal of 20 new customers. You can the importance of goal setting, writing goals down, and taking action it's a game changer.

This is GK adding to this chapter. Brad did a great job on giving you the outline on how to set your goals into action step by step. Let me now give you some more insight on goals. Out of the 20 takeover skills, goals are probably the one that almost everyone knows about. For some, it might be the only one they know about. Every New Year's we have people telling the world their goals for the new year. It sounds really simple, right? Write down what you want and go after it but somewhere between the writing it down and then going after it, it just doesn't happen for most people. They are left year after year believing that they're going to achieve these goals and it just never happens. Instead, they go through a lifetime without ever achieving their goals.

I look at goal setting like baking a cake. There are quite a few ingredients. Flour is the main ingredient, say, but without the other key ingredients, the cake would never bake correctly or taste right. This is the issue with goal setting. Goal setting is just one aspect of a recipe. This is the reason why we wrote *The Takeover* – we know you need all the ingredients to achieve what you want.

I find it amazing that most people go through their entire life without someone sharing the success skills needed for the best possible with them. I wonder how someone can live their entire life not knowing the principles that create success? I didn't know until I was 40 years old that on an aluminum foil container, if you poke the perforated holes on both ends of the aluminum foil box, it keeps it from falling out. I actually taught that lesson to my fiancé, as she didn't know it either. We were both amazed as silly as it sounds. Did you know this about aluminum foil? You don't have to tell me. As you see, just on a small-scale example, we somehow go through life so busy that we don't search for knowledge. This needed knowledge for success will never just come to us. It's our responsibility to search in life. If you're a treasure hunter, you're never going to have a treasure come to you, you have to search for the treasure. We can't sit back and wait for that big break in life, we must set it up so that we run into it. Will Smith didn't sit at home and magically become a famous actor. No, he went out and searched for the knowledge to become who he is today. Nobody was coming to look for him; he went out and found success.

Every year I have new goals, but they don't necessarily start on January 1. They start the actual year before. As I'm working on my current goals for the year, I already see a year ahead, sometimes 2 to 5 years ahead on what I need to accomplish. I'm setting myself up stage by stage to get to the ultimate goal. Of course, life is throwing roadblocks I don't expect but when all the skills in this book are working in harmony, you can overcome any challenge and get back up and still accomplish the goal regardless if it might take a little bit longer or even a lot longer. Once you know you're going to do something, and nothing is stopping you don't care what life throws at you because you know it's part of the process. Once you decide that your goals are no longer a choice and it is part of your DNA integrated into your life regardless of circumstances, you'll soon be a force to be reckoned with.

Now I'm going to keep it transparent with you because I always do. I'm not perfect seven days a week, but my goal on a daily basis is to win the majority of the days in a week and in the month. If something comes up and let's say I lose a whole week of production, I compact the remaining time left of the year to make up for that loss. Personally, I have less leisure time than most. Therefore, my goals get accomplished much faster than most people do. This allows me for that makeup time if needed throughout the year.

My philosophy is I put the time into it now to get the time back later when it counts. So, what is the difference between just goal setting and gold utilization? Goal setting is saying what you want to do without the proper skills and understanding of how to see the goal through. Goal utilization is having all the ingredients ready and utilizing them in harmony, mentally rehearsing the obstacles and making a decision that the goal will be accomplished as nothing will stand in your way. You have no choice!

The key points – Goal setting is something very practical that anyone can do. First, you must visualize what it is that you want and know exactly what you want. Your goals must be vividly imagined and ardently desired. Desire is like the ether that fuels your goals and will push you on the days that you are not motivated. Depending on where you are at on your journey, you must make the appropriate adjustments on how you are setting your daily "Critical Tasks". You must write your goals down on paper and read them aloud daily and nightly and do everything in your power to every task completed before the day is over.

Keep in mind that if you can create the habit writing your goals out and down on paper the night before you will wake up in the morning with the sense of purpose and a great sense of direction on how you were going to attack and win the day. Also, keep in mind what bonds all this together is discipline. You must be disciplined to write your goals down every day and then take action! Lastly, understand all the ingredients are key to optimization of achievement of goals. Setbacks are part of the winning process. The choice to not quit ultimately gets you there in the end.

TAKEOVER 15

YOUR WORD

Brad here, so what does it mean to keep your word? It essentially means you are going to do what you say you will do. It's not rocket science. However, this is something that is easily overlooked and broken on a daily basis. Why? Overpromising. Fear of telling people no. Were you sidetracked by other events? Or was it that you forgot or just simply didn't do what you said that you were going to do. This is where your character and integrity are put to the test.

I must have been about seven or eight years and I remember my mother telling me and my two sisters that my dad was coming up from Maryland to pick us up. Now just so you can understand this a little bit better, I was the only boy living in a house with all women. Finally!!! I felt like I had some backup coming for TEAM BOYS!! I remember getting ready the night before. My outfit was laid out, my sneakers were nice and clean, and my dad was coming, and I wanted to make sure that everything was perfect. I was so excited to see him, so I patiently waited on the front porch, anticipating his arrival. An hour went by and still no dad. Two hours went by and still nothing. My mom finally came out and gave me the devastating news. "Hey, your dad's not going to be able to make it today, honey." All I could remember was our last conversation of my dad saying that he would be there. I was crushed and heartbroken. I want you to remember the 7 and 8-year-old version of you next time you give someone your word. You may get away with letting someone down once or twice. But the consequences can be deep, and you may never know the effects that it has on others.

The consequences of breaking your word can be very serious. You will slowly start to lose the trust of everyone around you which will absolutely damage your reputation. Words have meanings and you must protect your words at all cost. When we tell someone that we are going to do something we create a certain expectation. Every time you break your word you are essentially telling the world, I am not a person you can trust. There was one personal rule that I maintained and upheld my whole life – if I cannot trust you, I cannot do business or be friends with you. That rule is set in stone in my book.

Let's talk about one of the most important "words" to keep and follow through with, it is your word when you tell yourself you're going to do something. This right here has been one of the key ingredients in personal growth and development. Saying and telling yourself that you are committed to doing something and then you do it. Most people have heard this one before. I'm going to start the gym on Monday or I'm going to quit smoking on

January 1. We see this over and over again where people cannot even commit to the word that they gave themselves. The same rules apply if you were to give your word to another person – if you tell yourself you're going to do something, do it.

I feel confident that everyone understands what the negative ripple effect can be by not keeping your word in your personal life and your professional life. Let's talk about all the positive things that can happen when you do keep your word. Keeping your word will build trust, integrity, confidence and will ultimately shape your character in the perception of what people think and know of you and more importantly what you think, know and believe of yourself. People will start to gravitate towards you and your purpose in life.

GK here – through the climb to top income earner in the network marketing industry and as a successful real estate investor, I have learned how important keeping your word is to self-growth. It was actually surprising to me the number of people I have interacted with that do not keep their word in life. Countless times, I've had people reach out to me expressing they want to change their lives and how they want to meet with me to earn more money. When it came time to meet, they either had a last-minute excuse or they went into the witness protection program and were never heard from again. I think these people go through life not understanding how important it is to respect another person's time.

It also shows that you don't value people when you don't keep your word. Telling a person one thing and doing another doesn't help the growth of your character or integrity in a positive direction. In many cases, the dreaded fear kicks in or someone in their circle influence discourages them from trying something new. The fearful of change kicks in and not only do they give up their attempt to be better they also skip out on their word. The unknown is scary to most people so rather than face the unknown they back out of their commitment. We live in a world now where we can easily avoid interaction by sending a text message or blocking someone online to escape our own shortcomings.

As a real estate investor, I was having the same experience. I currently own 34 rental units. As they become vacant, I place ads to find occupancy for them. It's very easy to find tenants but in the process, I come across quite a few people who do not keep their word. Every single time, there will be at least 1 to 2 dozen individuals to contact me stating how bad they want the apartment. They say they will give me cash when we meet before even seeing it. And every single time, 80% of the people who set the appointment and confirmed the night before either cancel the morning of it with an excuse, don't send a message to cancel, or don't apologize for not being able to make their appointment.

I won't even get into the reasons that people don't pay their rent on time. That can be a whole chapter itself. Not showing up in life and ignoring people is a definite way to not get ahead in life. Energy attracts energy. You'll always attract the type of energy you display.

And really, do you really want to do business with someone who can't keep their word? Can you trust someone who can't be straightforward with you? Don't get me wrong, things happen where people can't keep their commitments, but those people respectfully communicate and reschedule and respect your time. I've taught myself to not allow either of these 2 situations to ever take me out of my element or slow me down.

I've made a promise to myself to do my best to never allow someone else's behavior to affect my inner peace. Many of the individuals who do not keep their word, if I am able to follow their life on social media, I see that five years later they're in the same position financially and have the same level of self-growth and still are complaining about life. Keeping your word is huge, as it shows the level of integrity you have and what type of character you're developing. It lets people know they can count on you and that you're always going to do what you say.

Successful people that I associate with don't have the patience for those who do not keep their word. In the end, if you're consistently not keeping your word, you'll burn through your good contacts in life very quickly. People will never want to do business with you or at times even associate with you if you're like this. We have all most likely heard the expression "my word is my bond". At the end of our lives, nothing else we have accumulated will truly matter but our word will. People will remember us for what we said and if we did what we said. If you're someone who doesn't keep their word, then today is a new start. You can always re-brand yourself and make a change that people will see and believe in.

Here are a few ways to keep your word and rebrand yourself. Make fewer promises than you do. Learn to only make promises which you can keep. Don't agree to something that you don't want to do. Just man up and say no! Completely eliminate excuses from your life. Be self-aware and stop making them excuses. Stop being vague with your words. You either do or you don't, there is no try. Make sure to fulfill your commitments quickly. Make it a standard to always follow through, because you said you would and unless is absolutely unavoidable, always show up and conquer that little voice that is telling you not to.

The key points – keeping your word is one of the most important things you will need to learn to do. Success can be lost at any time in life. We all know stories of successful people who did things unethical and lied to achieve success. Once successful they continued to only think about themselves and in the end lost it all. It is of the utmost importance to be self-aware on keep your word. It's mandatory to keep people's image of you in a positive light as someone who always comes through and can be counted on. Also, someone that values other people's lives and their time. Mastering these takeover tools and being a person of integrity will have the world wanting to do business with you. Take it from us; we now get most of our best opportunities from people coming to us.

We built a brand based on our word. That makes us stand out and hence people trust us. Therefore, everything goes smoother and walls are broken down because of the reputation of our word. If you can't keep your word for an important reason, make sure you're honest and make the other party feel valued. And be the one to make the effort for the next encounter. We suggest even going out of your way. The bottom line is that your word is your bond. At the end of your life, there won't be a U-Haul with all your stuff at your viewing. What will be seen and heard are the people talking about you as a person. One of the best life compliments will be he/she always kept their word and you could always count on them to come through.

TAKEOVER 16

COMPOUND EFFECT

I remember being a personal trainer and sitting down with my client for the first time doing a very simple needs assessment. I would always ask them this question "how do you think you got to where you're at right now?" and most of my clients would look at me distressed and say "I don't know, I don't know how I got there". Most of my clients were with me to lose weight, look better, and feel better, but when I asked them that question, they could never give me a definitive answer. The reality of it was quite simple. It was the compound effect of all the little things that they were doing in their life. From what their diet consisted of, to how much they were exercising on a weekly basis even breaking it down to how much water you're consuming on a daily basis.

Most people don't notice when they gain 2 pounds but if you are consistently gaining 2 pounds every two months over the course of five years, you will end up being 60lbs overweight. Now if you gained 60 pounds over 2 months, you would be in shock, but you didn't gain it overnight; it was accumulating over a long period of time. It was a sweet treat here, some fast food there – it all adds up. You miss one day of exercise that turns into a week that turns into a month. I knew exactly how my client got to where they were. It just needed to be broken down, it's a very bite-size piece for them to understand what the compound effect is.

Now, this same process can happen with your finances, it can happen with your career or business. This is a very remedial concept. The small choices that you make day in and day out over a long period of time ultimately add up to your overall results. Like I said earlier, you're not going to notice the 2 pounds every other month. But know that every time you lose the discipline to do what you know you're supposed to do, it adds to the negative compound effect. In the same flip of the coin, have confidence that every time that you maintain your discipline you will have a positive result on the compound effect.

George writing here. The compound effect is the takeover skill that will sneak up on you and have you wondering how your life got to where it's at. Or you'll master it and wake up five years from now living the reality you've always wanted. For many years, I went through life not understanding that it's not the big things that get you ahead in life – it's the little unnoticeable things. If you take a look at your life today, most likely there isn't one major event that has you in the situation you're currently in. Alas, it comes from a series of small consistent things that you did over time that eventually compounded into something much bigger. As I got around people who taught me self-awareness and I studied my own past, I started to recognize a reoccurring pattern.

Self-awareness must be present to even see the compound effect of your actions. That's why this book is specifically designed to give you everything you need in order to succeed. I recognized the pattern of small choices daily that in time dictated my unfavorable results. Our results never come for us just wanting them. Life will never give you what you want, it gives you what you deserve. The result always comes from a series of actions that over a period of time. You're either compounding forward or backward – nothing stays the same. So, just stating that I want to change my life or I want to be wealthy or I want to be successful won't work if on a daily basis, the small stuff I do is compounding in the wrong direction.

Every morning I go over my daily activities, whether it's what meetings I have or who I have to meet. I then ask myself, is what I'm doing pushing me forward for keeping me where I'm at? I realize in life that most things are easy to do but it just but just as easy not to do. I can tell you the first time I made 100k a year it was no harder than making 35k a year before. It was the same amount of time, 24 hours a day. When my self-awareness was being utilized effectively and I was fully aware of the compound effect at all times, my results tripled in the same 24 hours. Once you master the compound effect, it starts to build momentum. I can tell you from my experience that whether it's going from 100k to 500k a year or going from 5 rental units to 20th rental units it's not any harder to achieve. You will just have more responsibilities but that's part of the molding process and why we wrote this book. Every new level you reach will need an updated version of you. But if you understand the compound effect, you'll be aware of what life is giving you daily and you'll be ready. Start making your small decisions towards a positive direction and over time, I'll see you in the winner's circle.

The key points – what you need to take away about the compound effect is that what you do repeatedly day to day, week to week, month to month, year to year… it will all add up. The little decisions that you make every day will have a very significant impact on your life. You're either compounding forward or backward, no one stays the same. Keep in mind that these decisions are 100% yours. You have to own it. Think about the ripple effect that all of your daily decisions are going to have long-term in your life. Start making the little positive decisions that will have a positive compound effect on your life one year from now, two years from now, 10 years from now. Use the compound effect to your advantage!!

TAKEOVER 17

OBJECTIVES AND PROBLEMS

It was February 5th, 2006. The Seattle Seahawks versus the Pittsburgh Steelers. Those of you that are football fans know that this was Superbowl XL. The Steelers were losing going into halftime. The Steelers defensive line was being picked apart, on top of the Seahawks offense was completely dialed in. I am a firm believer that there are two primary reasons why the Steelers ultimately won the Super Bowl that year. Focusing on objectives and playing to win. I have told the story countless times in training and developing my sales and management teams over the past 17 years. There was a very important lesson to be learned that day. Prior to halftime, the Steelers were in disarray. They were not making simple plays, they were not communicating, and from the sidelines, it looked as if they were playing based on "how not to lose".

They had problem after problem. It was not looking good for Coach Cowher and his Steelers. I actually had a chance to witness the pivotal point in that game. At that time, I do not think most people didn't really grasp what was going on. The camera focused on Jerome "The Bus" Bettis, one of the greatest halfbacks of all time, as the camera zoomed in on Jerome, it showed him pacing up and down the bench where are all of Steelers players were sitting down on the bench. The whole bench had their heads hanging low, looking defeated, players arguing, and it looked as if the team had lost all of their energy. Heck, it looked as if they had already lost the game. As Jerome was walking up and down the bench, he noticed the body language coming from his team.

All of a sudden, he smacks one of his teammates in the helmet, he hits another player on the shoulder pads then he started to walk up and down the line physically, making every one of his teammate's stand up. He even grabbed one of them from under the chin as if he was telling them to hold their head up; I was witnessing a leader reframing the thought process of his peers. Up until that point of the game, the Steelers were concentrating on their problems instead of their objective and once they put their eye back on the ball, no pun intended, they started to focus on their objectives and started to "play to win".

My intent was to show you that it does not matter if you are a high school student reading this or a professional football player, the principles will always remain the same. To win the game, you must focus and put all of your energy into the objective. That is how you win. Earlier in this book, GK and I covered TAKEOVER 4, MIND CONTROL and the importance of it. These two chapters, in a way, go hand in hand. You have to control your thought process when you are challenged or are dealing with adversity and problems. If you choose to focus and put more energy into your problem, guess what's going to happen. Yep! Your problems will only grow, and they will become bigger problems. If you do the opposite and put your focus and energy into the objective and the solutions that will get you to accomplish the goal, in most cases, that is how you win.

Most people will spend as much as 90% of their time talking and focusing on their problems which will in turn influence 10% of their productivity. Those are terrible statistics for anyone that is actively working on creating a better life for themselves.

Think of yourself as a world-class championship boxer. I think it is safe to say that a world class boxer knows how to stay on their feet, think quickly, and take a punch. A punch to a boxer is a problem. How many problems is a boxer faced with in a 12-round match? Hundreds of them. When the boxer takes their first hit, do they run back to their corner and start crying to their team that they just got popped? Do they look out into the crowd looking for their significant other looking for a shoulder to cry on or do they pick up the phone and started calling all of their friends and tell them about their problems? Absolutely not!! The boxer will take the punch, make quick adjustments, and maybe change their stance or change their hit patterns. The prizefighter will immediately focus on the solutions and how they are going to win the fight. It is automatic. To all of you out there reading this, fight your problems head-on. Do not talk about them, fight them with action and solutions.

George writing here. One thing I've had to come to terms with is that regardless of the level of success that I achieve, the amount of money that I make or the amazing circle of influence I have, there will always be problems. The problems are just different on each level, but they are still problems. If anything, there is more responsibility which means more problems. I definitely have more problems at my level now than before but they simpler to handle. How's that? It's because I practice being solution-oriented and now it's part of my DNA and the only thing I know.

I've become a stronger version of myself, therefore, the stress hasn't changed, but I've changed. Problems are not the stress is the emotional response that we have to the problem that causes stress. You can minimize or even eliminate that stress if you decide just as I did a few years ago to no longer focus on the problem and always focus on the solution. Most people focus on the problem and that's all they know to focus on. It's been taught to them by their parents, friends, or peers. Focusing on the problem shuts your mind off from coming up with a solution.

All the successful people that I know become solution-oriented individuals. When there is an issue, they immediately think "what will fix this problem?" Being a real estate investor, I've had many problems. For example, a tenant calls me in a panic that a pipe froze and burst. In the past, my natural instinct was to get stressed and panic. Since I've had the mind shift to be solution-oriented, it has completely changed my reaction. I've known that it won't matter in a month. I know that there is a licensed plumber on my team that can handle it much better than me. That if I stay calm, my tenants will stay calm. When your mind is about solutions you find yourself having the right things in place so that when problems arise, the solutions are already there.

My advice for you is this – look at objections from people and problems from people as opportunities. Without problems, there is no opportunity, no growth, and no change. I've learned through hardships that everything happens for a reason. It's all happening to prepare you for what's coming. We may not see at the time it will make sense when you're looking back from the winner's circle. All of you reading this are most likely 6 to 18 months away from a major breakthrough. If you start to focus on solutions, that road will be much easier for you. Next time there is a problem, ask yourself "what is the solution?" and laser beam your focus onto that. I wish you all the best in your efforts!

The key points to objectives and problems are simple but still require effort and accountability on your end. Keep in mind that when you focus on your problems, they will almost always become bigger and you will never give it the time and attention that is needed for the solution. The same way that you could manifest and bring to life all of the positive things, is the same way that you can put energy and focus on all of the negative things.

Remember, be the boxer and fight your problems head-on and be super reactive with solutions every time you are faced with a problem or are dealing with a challenge. Always ask yourself, "what is the solution?" Keep in mind that your problems are an opportunity for you to become a better version of yourself.

TAKEOVER 18

GRATITUDE

When's the last time you went to bed and thought about all the things you're grateful for? When's the last time you woke up and were grateful to be alive? Gratitude is one of the main ingredients in living a purpose-driven life. It allows you to see the cup half full and not half empty. Everyone in my circle of influence who has created a better life practices gratitude. I've noticed that most people tend to focus on what they don't have in their life. Many even obsess on the missing pieces of the puzzle of life rather than what pieces they already have. Once you change your mental view from what you don't have to what you do have, you then realize you have more than you thought you did. It's easy to get caught up in life and see what everyone around you has and want the same but you realize, you're better off than many of the people in this world.

I, GK, can honestly say I went through an entire decade without true gratitude. I always focused on what I didn't have and how unfair life was to me and how some people had it better than me. It wasn't until I got around individuals who practiced being grateful with intent that I stopped dwelling on the shortcomings in my life. I realized they were happy because of their focus on the blessings they currently had. Sometimes, I run into somebody who has it way harder than me in life, whether it's battling cancer, losing a loved one, or dealing with an injury in which they can never walk again or just born somewhere where the opportunities are not as flourishing as they are here in America. When this situation arises, it's a serious gratitude check, but if these are the only times that we have a serious gratitude check, it will never be enough to program our mind to be more grateful. We will just occasionally have random days of gratitude. Without a system of intent, change cannot exist.

Today is that day that you will stop focusing on what your lacking and stop complaining life isn't fair. You'll start to be grateful for what you have. You'll have self-awareness and always remind yourself that there is always someone else in life that would trade places with you in a heartbeat. I guarantee you most people on their death bed if given the chance to trade places with you, would be grateful and embrace it all with happiness. It's all about perception and perception is a reality. Every night before going to sleep, I evaluate my day. I talk to myself about the things or people that I'm grateful for in my life. I pick at least three things even if they are seemly insignificant that day. Doing this for me allows me to rest better and it resets my brain for the new day ahead. Even if it's been the worst day ever, I make sure that before I sleep, I give my gratitude to my maker for the gift of life.

Being grateful in your social life is also important to your success. I make sure that I don't neglect letting the people in my life know how grateful I am for them being in it.

Whether is a significant other, child, parent, co-worker, business partner of anyone who's a positive part of life... gratitude goes a long way and it's contagious, it's time for you to start sharing gratitude with yourself and others. I didn't have the father-son relationship in my life that I wanted. For many years I focused on that and I was angry, but one day I decided because of my studies in self-development that I would focus on gratitude for who I became. And if my life was any different, I wouldn't be who I am. I wouldn't be writing this book most likely. So, I became grateful for the lack of that relationship. It sounds crazy to be grateful for the lack of having your father in your life but again perception is a reality. I also became grateful for the sheer fact that my dad was even alive and well to create me and give me this opportunity called life. Please start today to be thankful for what you have and start to practice gratitude as a system. Soon, you'll see your perception of your current situation dramatically change almost overnight.

This is Brad on the topic of being grateful. What GK just explained was a very simple and is an "easy to do" process in retraining your thought process in operating from a point of gratitude and appreciation. First thing when you wake up, think about all the great things in your life. FYI, if you woke up at all, that should be gratitude enough... just saying. But seriously, look at all the positive things that you have in your life. Now I'm not saying that what you have is ultimately what you want that is why you are working on improving yourself to get to where you want but be grateful for the simple things that you have. Your health, your family, if you're reading this book your head of a lot of people in this world already. Then do that exact same process as you were lying in bed going to sleep.

When I got in trouble, I lost everything. I lost my cars, I lost my motorcycle, I lost my money, I lost my friends, and I lost the life that I had at that time. It wasn't until that time that I had to check myself and realize that I was still alive, I had the ground under my feet and air in my lungs and my family was safe. It wasn't as bad as I thought it was. It sucked, but I was grateful for how everything turned out. The summer of the year that I got in trouble, I had four friends lose their lives due to their lifestyle and the way we were all living. I remember thinking about how grateful I was that I got in trouble. If not, I could have easily been the fifth person to lose their life. Most of the time you just must put things into perspective and see it from a different window and give thanks daily.

The key points – We often forget to be grateful. We tend to focus on what we don't have in life, and this behavior leaves us feeling unfulfilled. To change our perception and move forward to the life we want, we need to start practicing gratitude over and over. We must go through life thankful and always remembering someone else always has it worse. Remember that gratitude must become a habit. We are grateful for you reading this book and sharing the knowledge with others. Let's change your life and the lives of others for the better. Most importantly, be grateful that you woke up alive and healthy and you're are reading this book.

TAKEOVER 19

SELF AWARENESS

This is GK talking about the takeover skill self-awareness. For me, it's the one skill that changed my life the most. Creating self-awareness didn't start for me until I was made aware of it, no pun intended. Sounds crazy, right? I wasn't self-aware of self-awareness until I became aware through someone who had mastered it. I remember thinking, how is it that no one ever taught me this? My parents, my teachers, and my peers never said anything to me about it. Maybe this is the first time you're hearing about it. Or maybe it's the first time you really investigated it deeper. If I can leave you with anything in this book, just remember self-awareness will always keep you on track even if you fall off.

As I'm writing this book while doing the stationary bike at the gym, there is a woman next to me talking to me about her knee being sore. I politely answer her and then I keep writing on my phone. She then says, "when you're done with that, I wanted to ask you something". So, I tell her I'm an author and I'm writing my second book. She asked me "what is your book about?" I tell her it's a book about accountability, habits, goal setting, it's a self-help book.

She says to me that nobody out there will understand anything of what that means. I was blown away because that's the exact reason why I'm writing this book. I answered her by telling her only a small percent of people will understand this book probably about 5%. The movers and the shakers, as it were. Those who are entrepreneurs, business owners and people of influence that are making a difference in the world. She nodded her head as if to say "yes" in agreement. I felt I met her for a reason to validate this chapter. I now wanted to ask her name and her age because I wanted to know her better. I could tell she was probably around my grandmother's age. She tells me her name is JoAnn and was very adamant on the spelling and that she was 76 years old. I told her she looked great for her age and she smiled, which made me happy.

So, if you're reading this consider yourself more fortunate than most. This is a perfect example of an individual who's lived almost their entire life and never was taught any of the takeover tools that you're being taught in this book. Could you imagine how different her life could have been if she had read a book like this in her 20s, 30s, 40s, 50s, or even her 60s? I can't even say she would have wanted her life to be any different and maybe her life was amazing the way it was. But if she was exposed to self-development at least she could of have had another choice fulfilled a dream that maybe she never did. It's never too late but the longer you go not exposing your mind to these type of self-help skills, the harder it gets to break that already-programmed conscious mind.

What exactly is self-awareness? It's about consciously knowing every decision you make, and understanding that everything you do is important, even the little stuff. It's the little stuff that is the most important. It's the little stuff that causes the hardest life. If you have a tooth cavity and you don't take care of it, down the road you'll be paying for an expensive root canal. If your alignment is off on your car, you'll eventually need new tires costing you more than just an alignment. If your diet is bad over time, you'll need money for new clothes. Everything has a cost and the cost is always associated with the level of self-awareness. Most people get up and just go through the motions in life never understanding why there are even making decisions that they're making. They never audit their thoughts.

I once heard someone say that the hardest decision in a human being's life is the decision to conquer one's own self. That was so powerful that I realized from that point on I had to in a sense step outside of my own mind… that every thought or decision I made from that point on, my self-awareness would always audit my thoughts. I would ask is this right choice for the life that I want? Will this choice get me closer to where I want to be? Is this what someone more successful than me would do? What consequences will I possibly experience? Remember, everything we do either closes the gap from where we are to where we want to be or furthers it.

I urge all of you to put a filter on your thoughts. Ask yourself questions about your choices. You must realize when something must change in your life. People ask me sometimes why don't you wear a coat when it's freezing out? It's because that is when I'm the most self-aware that I'm alive. Being cold and having all my body shiver, reminds me that I'm still here, I still have time and I need to make the most of it. It may sound bizarre but that's what is my reminder during the Pennsylvania winters when it's easy to slow down and regress. Ultimately, my most powerful weapon is my self-awareness. It will take time but start today and add that audit system to your mind and everything else will fall into place.

The key points – This is one of the most important tools that will give you the greatest chance of massive success. It is imperative that you understand the importance of monitoring your thoughts and actions. Without doing this, you may spend a life of being stuck and fully developing your true self. You must develop your own moral compass and what I mean by that is you must understand what your emotions are and why you are feeling what you are feeling and more importantly you have to link your emotions with your thoughts and actions. You must also understand that this compass is guided by your personal values and standards, we stated this multiple time through this book that all these topics will flow through to one another. Start with understanding your values and standards. You must take a very hard deep look at the person in the mirror. That little voice in the back of your head has been telling you that there are things that you know you must do, take action and do it. Be self-aware. If you know that you got to lose a couple of pounds, eat healthier, and be aware. It's that simple. Do this, make sure you switch your mind auditor on, and watch your life unfold in the direction that you desire.

TAKEOVER 20

TRUST THE PROCESS

Yellow footprints. It was the night of November 28th, 1993. I was 17 years old, about to turn 18, and I was on a bus with about 60 other teenagers my age. It was dark, it was cold, and it was quiet. I remember asking myself over 100 times "how the hell did I get here?" I failed my senior year and dropped out of high school my second senior year and by this time I had been arrested at least four times. Then I heard "shut your mouths" and it brought me right back to reality. Not one of us spoke another word to each other, as instructed to. We finally made it to our destination, we pulled up outside of a red brick building and three men in camouflage came running on the bus screaming and yelling at the top of their lungs for all of us "maggots" to get off the bus and to go line up and put our feet on the yellow footprints outside.

This was the first step in the process of becoming a United States Marine. Every single man or woman that is in the United States Marines has experienced this exact same thing. Now, all of us were lined up on these yellow footprints and we were given very clear instructions as to what was about to happen in the next course of events. The one thing that was consistent that night was the yelling and screaming and the constant berating from our drill instructors; it seemed like they would never let up, from us stripping down into our skivvies to getting our heads shaved and having all of our uniforms issued to us. This infamous 13 weeks of misery and hell had just started, and I was going to become a Marine! In all of the years that I have been training and exercising this was hands-down the hardest training of my life. Marine Corps boot camp is definitely not a joke and up till this point my life I was pretty much on cruise control with life. I had absolutely no respect for the law nor any authority, and I pretty much did whatever the hell I wanted to.

Now I was on the polar opposite end of the spectrum. Being told what to do, how to do it, when to do it, and how long to do it. Constantly being pushed physically to the point of exhaustion. Every muscle in my body hurt. I was mentally exhausted too, what with being told over and over again that I should quit and go home, that I wasn't built for this, and constantly being questioned on why I was even there. Physically and mentally I was pushed to the brink of almost breaking down, but I wasn't alone, I had 60 brothers right by my side feeling the exact same feelings that I felt. Boot camp broke quite a few men. It didn't matter where you were from, it didn't matter what race you were, it didn't matter what religion you had, and it definitely didn't matter how much money you made. Marine Corps boot camp was a process that was designed to break you down, just like life itself.

I definitely didn't understand it as I was going through the pain and the suffering, but I will never ever forget my Drill Instructor Sgt. Brown the night before we graduated, the night before I officially became a United States Marine. He pulled me aside and he said "I hope you understand now why I was so hard on you... this was all part of the process" and he looked at me with this huge smile (which we rarely saw unless he was beating the snot out of one of us) and winked.

At the beginning of boot camp, we were taught the basics. How to put on a uniform, how to march, how to break down an M-16. When it came to the physical activity, again the basics. Running, push-ups, sit-ups, pull-ups. They were creating a foundation for us to be mentally and physically strong. Every stage through Boot Camp was designed to give us certain levels of experience and confidence to prepare us for the next stage. This process was repeated multiple times until it broke us, or we became Marines.

I reflect on this time in my life quite often because it will always help me remember that there is and there will continue to be a process in my own personal growth and development. This goes for all of you as well. You may not understand why you are going through the pain and suffering right now and I'm sure that there are so many of you that deal with the struggle of self-doubt. I still deal with self-doubt and this is simply due to the fact that I am still growing and progressing to the next stage of my life.

What GK and I want to accomplish with this book is the same thing that my drill instructor did with me at the beginning of Boot Camp, we want to break it down to the basics. We want you to understand the basic components of self-development and personal growth so we lined out 20 "Nuggets" that can give you the core foundation to chase your dreams and live the life that you ultimately want. These are proven facts that work as long as you are disciplined to be conscious of every single one. Being able to trust this process of your personal growth takes discipline, effort and most importantly personal accountability.

This is GK writing here. Would you have a better chance of winning the Super Bowl with the New England Patriots or the worst team in the league? This is an obvious answer. Does having Tom Brady guarantee you'll always win? No, but you're going to win more often than none. The 2018 record of the New England Patriots wasn't their best, but they trusted the process and still ended up super bowl champions. Trusting The process is a belief that throughout the entire journey you know it will end in your favor. Having all the takeover tools at your disposal gives you the best chance of winning the game that counts – the end game. There will be times where the challenge becomes overwhelming and you're at the brink of exhaustion and you're ready to throw in the towel, but it's these moments when everyone else chasing the same dream quits.

It's also this moment that the winners competing with you for the same life don't quit. You need to remember this when you get no situations that this is the critical moment that most people quit. It can take 10 years before you have a breakthrough year but without the skills to success that we taught you in this book your chances of surviving the punches life throws at you along the way are slim to none. You now have a better understanding of what to expect as you're pushing forward to reach your final desired destination. As you evolve, the challenges evolve. You can never stop learning more skills. Brad and I are devoted to your success and as we learn more along the climb, we will produce *The Takeover 2*.

What Will be in that book? We actually don't know yet, but we do know that there be more knowledge to obtain to continue furthering our levels of success. And yes, we will share that knowledge with you as we are committed to helping as many people as we can reach. You must trust yourself and the process! It's going to be hard at times, but anything worthwhile is hard. Remember, anyone can be a nobody but it takes courage and trust in one's own self to be a somebody. If it was easy everyone would be reading this book, and everyone would be out there chasing their dreams. You're not everybody, your different and it's time for you to shine bright, let's get it!

The key points – Along the road to success you'll want to quit – this is inevitable. For some, there will be multiple instances of wanting to throw in the towel. There will be times it feels too hard, you don't believe you can do it and even at times questions your sanity. Every successful person has gone through a roller coaster of emotions to get to the top. But the fact is that you must trust the process! Understand that what you're going through is normal and others have experienced it and conquered it. If they can do it, you can do it. There is no other way around it. Keep the commitment you made to yourself and others and don't stop until you win. Commitment is doing what you said you were going to do long after the feeling you said it in is gone.

At this moment Brad and I would like to thank you for reading our book. We appreciate everyone who is intertwined with our lives in this thing we call "life". It is now time for a call to action.

You must take all that you have learned from these 20 Takeover skills and have the biggest and best leap forward in many different aspects of your life. We believe in you 100% and can't wait to hear your story of success as you get to the next level.

Feel free to reach out to us; we look forward to hearing from you! We want to leave you with these 2 thoughts before you dive off into the mind exercises. Positive things happen to positive people who take positive action. First, there is a thought, your thoughts create feelings, your feelings create actions, and actions create habits over time.

Soon enough, your habits will give you your end result.

Mind Training Exercises

Here are some ways that successful people simply change their thoughts to dramatically change the outcome of a situation.

INSTEAD OF		TRY THINKING
I'M NOT GOOD AT THIS	>>>	WHAT AM I MISSING?
THIS IS NEVER HAPPENING	>>>	I'M ON THE RIGHT TRACK
I GIVE UP	>>>	WHAT STRATEGIES CAN I USE?
THIS IS TOO HARD	>>>	THIS MAY TAKE TIME AND EFFORT
I MADE A MISTAKE AND FAILED	>>>	MISTAKES ARE OPPORTUNITIES TO LEARN
I WILL NEVER BE AS SMART/TALENTED/SUCCESSFUL AS X	>>>	I'M GOING TO FIGURE OUT HOW X DOES IT AND LEARN FROM THAT
IT'S GOOD ENOUGH	>>>	IS IT REALLY MY BEST WORK?
PLAN A DIDN'T WORK	>>>	WHAT'S PLAN B OR C?

Now let's look at examples of how successful people change their thinking and elimate their limiting beliefs by converting them into empowering beliefs.

LIMITING BELIEFS		EMPOWERING BELIEFS
I AM A VICTIM OF CIRCUMSTANCE	>>>	I CREATE MY OWN REALITY
LIFE HAPPENS TO ME	>>>	LIFE HAPPENS FOR ME
I LIVE IN SCARCITY – THERE'S NEVER ENOUGH	>>>	I LIVE IN ABUNDANCE –THERE'S ALWAYS ENOUGH
OBSTACLES HOLD ME BACK	>>>	OBSTACLES HELP ME GROW
I CAN'T START UNTIL ____ HAPPENS	>>>	STARTING BEFORE I'M READY LEADS TO SUCCESS
THIS IS TOO HARD, I SHOULD QUIT	>>>	IF IT WAS EASY, EVERYONE WOULD BE DOING IT
I HAVE A BAD PAST	>>>	MY PAST IS WHAT SHAPED ME TODAY

SUGGESTED READING LIST

Here are the top 5 books for each of us that had the biggest impact on our lives :

GK's top 5 list

1. The Charge – *Brendon Buchard*
2. The Magic of Thinking Big – *David J. Schwartz*
3. The Subtle Art of Not Giving a Fu** – *Mark Manson*
4. The Slight Edge – *Jeff Olson*
5. Key to Yourself – *Venice J Bloodworth*

Brad's top 5 list

1. Think & Grow Rich – *Napoleon Hill*
2. 21 Irrefutable Laws of Leadership – *John C. Maxwell*
3. The Success Principles – *Jack Canfeild*
4. Extreme Ownership – *Jacko Willink & Leif Babin*
5. How to Make Sh*t Happen – *Sean Whalen*

Here are the top 5 podcasts that we get the most value from:

GK's top 5 list

❶ The Bigger Pockets – *Brandon Turner, David Greene*

❷ Cardone Zone – *Grant Cardone*

❸ The GaryVee Audio Experience – *Gary Vaynerchuk*

❹ The Create Your Own Life Show – *Jeremy Ryan Slate*

❺ Entrepreneurs on Fire – *John Lee Dumas*

Brad's top 5 list

❶ The MFCEO Project – *Andy Frisella*

❷ The Ed Mylett Show – *Ed Mylett*

❸ Jocko Podcast – *Jocko Willink*

❹ Impact Theory – *Tom Bilyeu*

❺ The School of Greatness – *Lewis Howes*

42980303R00071

Made in the USA
Middletown, DE
19 April 2019